MADRONA

FIRST AMERICANS

The Haida

DAVID C. KING

Marshall Cavendish Benchmark
New York

ACKNOWLEDGMENTS

Series consultant: Raymond Bial

Marshall Cavendish Benchmark
99 White Plains Road
Tarrytown, New York 10591-9001
www.marshallcavendish.us

Text copyright © 2007 by Marshall Cavendish Corporation
Map and illustrations copyright © 2007 by Marshall Cavendish Corporation
Map and illustrations by Christopher Santoro

All rights reserved. No part of this book may be reproduced or utilized in any form or by any means electronic or mechanical, including photo-copying, recording, or by any information storage or retrieval system, without permission from the copyright holders.

All Internet sites were available and accurate when sent to press.

Library of Congress Cataloging-in-Publication Data
King, David C.
The Haida / by David C. King.
p. cm. — (First Americans)
Includes bibliographical references and index.
ISBN-13: 978-0-7614-2250-1
ISBN-10: 0-7614-2250-1
1. Haida Indians—History--Juvenile literature. 2. Haida Indians—Social life and customs—Juvenile literature. I. Title. II. Series:
First Americans (Benchmark Books (Firm)
E99.H2K56 2006
979.8004'9728—dc22
2006011969

Photo research by Joan Meisel
Cover photo: Dewitt Jones/Corbis
Art Resource, NY: 7, 15, 22, 23, 32, Werner Forman; Corbis: 1, 12, 28, 36, 39 Dewitt Jones; 16, 30, Werner Forman; 18, Canadian Museum of Civilization; 26, Gary Braasch; Getty Images: 33, 34; Raymond Bial: 4; The Granger Collection, NY: 11, 14.

Editor: Tara T. Koellhoffer
Editorial Director: Michelle Bisson
Art Director: Anahid Hamparian
Series Designer: Symon Chow

Printed in China
1 3 5 6 4 2

CONTENTS

1. **The People and the Land** — 5

2. **The Haida Way of Life** — 13

3. **Beliefs and Ceremonies** — 27

4. **The Haida Today** — 37

Time Line — 42
Glossary — 44
Find Out More — 46
Index — 48

1 · THE PEOPLE AND THE LAND

On the west coast of North America, a narrow strip of land stretches from northern California to present-day Alaska. Hemmed in by the snowcapped peaks of the Pacific Coast Ranges, it is somewhat cut off from the rest of North America. Native American tribes known as the Northwest Coast Indians built thriving villages in this area. One of these societies, the Haida, lived on the coast of present-day Alaska. Like their neighbors, the Haida developed a remarkable way of life that was very different from other North American cultures.

Although the Haida never grew crops or raised farm animals, they acquired far more food than they needed by fishing, hunting, and gathering wild foods. In fact, they had so much food that they did not need to fish or hunt during the winter. Instead, they spent their time making beautiful objects out of wood and holding elaborate ceremonies and dances.

Warm ocean currents create milder winters on the coast than farther inland.

The Haida created their sophisticated way of life in an environment that seems harsh in many ways. The Coast Ranges tower 3,000 feet (914 m) on average above the narrow coastal strip. Thousands of years ago, glaciers pushed down from the mountains, carving a jagged coastline and creating lots of islands. Many Haida villages were built on one of the largest of the islands, known today as Prince of Wales Island. Cold mists and rains fall on the coastline during the long winter. The moisture helps thick forests of cedar, spruce, and pine to grow.

Although the Haida homeland is far north, the climate is surprisingly mild. In summer, the days

The Haida lived on the Pacific coast on land that is now part of the state of Alaska.

are cooled by the ocean, and in winter, a warm ocean current flows north along the coast, making the weather mild. The environment was inviting to the Indian tribes for other reasons: the sea and the rivers were full of fish, especially salmon, and the forests contained deer, bear, and other game, as well as a variety of berries, roots, and grasses. By 1600, about a hundred thousand people lived on the coast between present-day Alaska and Washington and Oregon. It was the most thickly settled region of North America.

Even without metal tools, the Haida built sturdy wood-plank houses.

Haida History

Like all Native American groups, the Haida trace their history back more than 20,000 years, when a bridge of land connected western Asia to the coast of Alaska. Historians believe that over many centuries, the ancestors of today's Indian tribes crossed that bridge and slowly spread out as they moved south.

By about 7500 b.c.e., some groups had settled along the northwest coast. The people lived by fishing, hunting, and gathering wild foods. By 6000 b.c.e., they were building canoes and houses of wood planks.

In the 1600s and 1700s, the first Europeans arrived. They brought a very different way of life, including powerful weapons such as guns and cannons and the belief that they should teach the Indians how to live like Europeans. English, Russian, and American traders were eager for furs, especially of sea otters, and this led to drastic changes in the Haida way of life. The men spent more and more time hunting sea otter to trade. This brought them new wealth, but before long, the sea otter almost vanished because of too much hunting.

European and American traders also brought diseases such as smallpox to which the Haida had no resistance. Entire villages were wiped out, and, by about 1800, the population of the Northwest Coast tribes was only about one-fifth of what it had been in 1600.

During the 1800s, pioneers from the United States and Canada wanted to take over the coastal lands and rivers for lumber, farming, fishing, and mining (especially for gold). The Haida and other tribes were gradually forced to move onto **reservations**—land set aside by the government. The Indians continued to fish and hunt, but the competition from newcomers steadily reduced the supply of animals and fish. In spite of promises from the Canadian and U.S. governments, the Haida had to depend on government charity to survive. After years of struggle, the life of all of the Northwest Coast tribes began to improve in the late 1990s.

The Haida Story of Creation

Many lifetimes ago, the Haida say, the world was occupied by the Animal People. They were giant beings who looked like animals but behaved like humans. Some were vicious and cruel, and some really were monsters.

One day, the Old One, who had created the Animal People, shaped some mud into the form of humans and breathed life into them. These first humans did not know how to survive, and the huge Animal People made their lives miserable. The Old One saw this and sent Coyote to help them. Coyote, who is also known as the Trickster, knew just what to do. He killed the monsters and found ways to shrink the other Animal People into the animals we know today. The only power the animals have now is to come back to life as food for humans.

In Haida myths, Moon Woman taught humans how to use plants.

2 · THE HAIDA WAY OF LIFE

The Haida depended on the sea, the rivers, and the forests for all their needs. During the summer months, they gathered nearly all of the food they needed to last them for the entire year.

Summer Work

Summer work was hard, but it was also fun. The men caught salmon in the river using a **weir**, a large net on poles strung across the river. As the men threw fish onto the grassy bank, the women gathered and cleaned them. Most of the salmon were placed on racks to dry. The women built fires under some of the racks to smoke the salmon. Smoked or dried salmon gave the villagers plenty of food for the cold, rainy months ahead. A few salmon were set aside for the day's meal, soaked in fish oil and eaten raw. The men caught other kinds of fish, including cod and halibut, but salmon were the most important part of the Haida's diet.

The Haida prepared seafood products for use throughout the year.

Sometimes, in the early morning, the women would walk along the beach, filling baskets with shellfish and seaweed. These foods were also saved for winter use.

Moving In

When the rainy season began, the Haida moved to their permanent homes. Sturdy wood-plank houses were clustered together close to the river. All of the houses faced the water,

The Haida built their villages in clusters near the water.

so the villagers would be able to see any enemy approaching.

Making houses was slow and difficult. The men pounded stone wedges into a crack in a log, slowly making the crack wider and deeper until a perfect plank split off. The planks were then tied to the foundation posts and crossbeams. Later the men stuffed moss between the planks to keep out the cold winds.

At last, the men put the great totem pole in place. It was beautifully carved and brightly painted. The carving at the top represented the family's clan. Other animal figures told the story of the **household**. Anyone who traveled on the

Totem poles tell the history of a family and clan.

Haida Government

Anyone who owned a dwelling was considered a house chief. A more important figure was the clan chief, whose position was based on his prestige—that is, people thinking highly of him. His prestige, in turn, depended more on his wealth than on his skill or courage in battle. The clan chief could pass his title on to his son as long as he had not given away most of his wealth.

This carved helmet belonged to a clan chief.

river could tell a lot about the families. At the bottom of the totem pole was an opening that formed the door to the house.

Inside the house were wooden sleeping platforms, which were kept snug against the walls. Around nine families lived in each house. Each had its own area, separated from the others by woven mats. In the center of the sand floor was a big fire for cooking and for heat. Smoke escaped through a hole in the roof.

The average house was about 40 feet (12 m) high and 30 feet (9 m) wide. With only one door and no windows, houses were dark and smoky.

The Haida tribe was separated into several clans. The clans were divided into households made up of a man, his wife or wives, their young children, their married daughters and their families, plus other relatives and several slaves.

Clothing

The Northwest Coast tribes were the only Indians north of Mexico to have wool. They did not raise sheep, but they got wool from mountain goats and from the fleece of a special breed of dogs called *wool dogs*. The wool, dyed bright colors, made wonderful blankets and cloaks. The Haida decorated the wool with beads, feathers, and bits of fur.

The women also stripped off the bark of young cedar trees, using sharp seashell scrapers. After the bark was soaked in saltwater for ten days, the women pounded it until they could pull the fibers apart. Then they wove the fibers into cloth.

Four chiefs display their richly decorated clothing.

This cedar cloth made soft blankets and capes that were warm and kept out the water. The cedar bark was also used for the cone-shaped hats that the Haida wore to keep off the sun in summer and the rain in winter.

Preparing Meals

Summer meals were easy because many foods were eaten raw or just soaked in fish oil. The Haida sometimes prepared dried roots and berries by pounding them into a grainy powder, adding water to make a dough, then forming the dough into small cakes.

Preparing meals with dried or smoked foods took time and skill. Dried salmon and other fish were soaked in water or fish oil to restore their moisture. Sometimes, the women baked the foods in a pit outside the house. Hot stones were placed in the bottom and the foods on top, often covered with seaweed to hold in the moisture. Boiled meals were prepared in the house, with the food cooked in a watertight box or basket. Seaweed or certain grasses made a saladlike side dish.

Recipe: Ground Nut Cakes

The Haida made small, dry cakes from many different foods, including thistles, berries, roots, and various kinds of nuts. Fish oil was commonly used to keep the dough moist and hold it together, but you might prefer the flavor of maple syrup. Be sure to have an adult help you with the oven.

Ingredients
- 1 cup ground nuts (such as almonds or walnuts)
- 1 teaspoon vanilla
- 1/2 cup maple syrup
- 1/2 cup flour
- 1 tablespoon cooking oil

Equipment
- nut grinder or blender
- mixing bowl and spoon
- cookie sheet
- adult helper

1. Preheat oven to 350 degrees. Ask an adult to help you use a nut grinder or blender to grind enough nuts to make 1 cup.
2. Stir in the vanilla and syrup. Add the flour and mix thoroughly to make a dough.
3. Form the dough into 1-inch balls. Spread a little cooking oil on the cookie sheet and place the cakes on the sheet.
4. Bake at 350 degrees for about 10 minutes until firm and lightly browned.

Makes 15 – 20 cakes

Woodworking

In the summer, when they weren't fishing, the men made canoes. Each canoe was made out of a single cedar log, hollowed out with stone tools. Some canoes were small and light, designed for two men to use for fishing or hunting. The largest canoes, measuring 70 feet (21 m), could hold about thirty to fifty men for an attack on an enemy. With a smaller crew of eight or ten, the large canoes were used to hunt sea mammals, including seals, sea otters, and even whales. The elegant, curved bow of the canoes showed the beauty of Haida woodworking, and also made the canoe easier to maneuver.

The Northwest Coast Indians had no knowledge of pottery, so they made objects out of wood instead of clay. Wooden bowls were expertly carved in the shape of canoes. Dinner bowls were about 12 inches (30 cm) long and feast dishes measured 3 to 4 feet (0.9 to 1.2 m). Other wood carvings included spoons, boxes, and small containers for fish oil. These items were often polished with sharkskin. Other objects were made out of horns and whale bones.

"Coppers"

The Haida made objects out of thin pieces of copper. The Haida got copper through trade with Indians who lived farther east and from European and American sailing ships that were wrecked along the coast. The **"coppers"** were hammered into elegant designs or engraved. Owners of coppers traded them, and, in time, the coppers became extremely valuable. A single copper could be worth 1,000 ceremonial blankets.

A beautifully designed copper plaque was used as a unit of wealth.

Haida men showed their greatest skill in making wooden boxes. They developed two special methods: bending and sewing. To bend a box, the craftsman first steamed the wood over boiling water, then used hot rocks to bend the corners. Holes were bored through the edges, and cedar twine was used to sew the pieces together.

Some of the most spectacular and colorful wood carving was done on totem poles. These tall poles were scattered throughout the village and served several functions. Some showed the history of a family; others were used as grave markers.

This bentwood box is painted with salmon designs.

Model Totem Pole

Haida woodworkers spent several months carving and painting a totem pole. They displayed great artistic skill in creating make-believe animals and birds. You can practice your creativity in this table model totem pole. *Remember to have an adult help you work with a knife.*

You will need:
- pencil and scrap paper
- ruler
- several sheets of newspaper
- block of balsa wood, 1 inch square and 5 inches long (available at craft stores)
- pen knife (you can even use a plastic picnic-set knife)
- ballpoint pen (black)
- crayons or colored pencils
- wood glue or craft glue
- scrap of thin plywood for a base, 4 to 5 inches square

1· Plan your totem pole on scrap paper. Draw a rectangle 1 inch wide and 5 inches long. Divide it into 1-inch squares, then plan an imaginary bird or animal for each square. Use the samples shown here or elsewhere in the book.

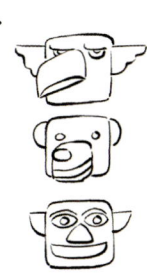

2· Spread newspaper on your work surface. Use the pencil and ruler to divide the balsa wood block into 1-inch squares. Have an adult help you cut away the corners to make it look like a stack of 5 separate blocks. Save the scraps you cut away.

3· Draw your animal and bird faces on one side of the totem pole. Go over the main features with black pen so they stand out. Use scraps of balsa wood to add details such as ears, noses, and beaks. Use crayons or colored pencils to add bright colors.

4· Glue the totem pole to the scrap of plywood for stability.

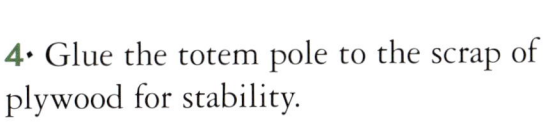

3 · BELIEFS AND CEREMONIES

The beliefs and customs of the Haida dealt with all phases of life. Every event, from infancy to old age, had special ceremonies and beliefs that helped people understand it.

The Life Cycle

Infancy. From the moment they were born, Haida infants were treated with great love and care. They were rubbed with whale oil and willow-ash powder, and wrapped in disposable diapers made of soft cedar bark cloth. For the first year, infants were kept in a **cradleboard**. The mother strapped the cradleboard to her back or propped it against a tree while she did her work.

The Haida believed that all unborn children lived in Babyland. There, they lived, played, and talked with other unborns. When an infant came to Earth, he or she still spoke Babyland language, which adults could not understand. Infants

Carved watchmen guard the top of a cemetery totem pole.

Children learned their adult roles by spending time with their parents.

who liked Earth would stay, but if an infant died, the Haida said the baby was not ready for Earth life yet and had gone back to Babyland.

Childhood. For their first five years, children spent a lot of time with their grandparents. The elders told them the tribe's stories and legends. At age six, children began to follow their parents, learning by watching them. Boys received their first lessons in fishing, hunting, and wood carving. Girls learned about housekeeping, weaving, and basketry.

The Vision Quest. When a boy was about thirteen years old, it was time for him to seek his special vision. He traveled alone into the wilderness and remained there for at least five days. Braving hunger, loneliness, the weather, and the danger of wild animals, he would pray to the Great Spirit to send him a vision. If he was fortunate, the vision of an animal or bird would come to him in a dream or a trance. The image of a grizzly bear might mean he would become a warrior, while an eagle vision meant he would someday be a chief. Some young men had to try several times before receiving their vision. The most unfortunate never had a vision and would never become leaders of the tribe.

The **vision quest** could also help a young man decide what he wanted to be. Certain jobs required long periods of training. A harpooner, for example, was not expected to do much more than use his special skill. The same was true of some wood-carvers, as well as healers, called **shamans**.

Marriage. Girls were considered ready for marriage when they were fourteen, boys at sixteen. Until then, boys and girls

Shamans

In all Northwest Coast societies, a small group of people had special powers for dealing with the spirit world. These were the shamans. They were the tribe's healers and were considered a special class. They even lived in a separate part of the village. When someone was so ill that the family's herbal medicine did not help, the shaman was called. He used his years of special training to create prayers and medicines, hoping to find a cure.

Every item on a shaman's necklace was believed to have special power.

had very little contact with each other. When a boy wanted to marry a girl, he went to her parents, not to the girl, and the wedding was arranged.

A wedding was a grand affair for the entire village. The father of the bride held a big party, with three or four days of feasting and dances. He also gave gifts to all the guests. Male guests then escorted the newly married couple to the shore, where they loaded the bridgroom's canoe with gifts.

A wealthy husband might take more than one wife, but usually not more than four. All of the wives recognized the first wife as primary, and all other wives had to come from the first wife's household.

Old Age and Death. The Haida treated the elderly with great respect, regarding them as the keepers of tribal history and records. When they stopped doing heavy work, they began to teach the young, reciting tribal stories and legends, and presiding at ceremonies. The elderly gave away most of their possessions, such as tools, canoes, and weapons, when they no longer needed them. Their personal property remained with them until they died.

The dead were usually placed in a box or canoe and tied high in a tree in the village cemetery. The name of the

Seeing an eagle during a vision quest meant a boy might become a chief. Here, a two-headed eagle decorates a chief's robe.

deceased was never spoken again. Otherwise, according to Haida beliefs, the spirit of the dead person might hear his or her name and try to return to life.

The Potlatch

One of the ceremonies of the Northwest Coast Indians was the **potlatch**, which has fascinated observers for many years. The potlatch was a ceremony in which a person gave away his possessions. The purpose of the potlatch was for a wealthy man or chief to show how important or generous he was by

The Haida showed great respect for the elderly members of their tribe.

giving away all of his wealth. The potlatch was also a way to challenge guests to display their own generosity and hospitality.

The whole family was involved in preparing the potlatch, an effort that might take several years. They wove blankets, carved masks, made baskets, and collected sea otter furs and deerskins. Food was prepared far ahead of time, because it was

Haida potlatch dancers pose for a photograph after a ceremony in 1901.

very important to have a lot more food than would be needed. Few things were more humiliating to the Haida than running out of food.

The potlatch consisted of singing, dancing, and games, as well as almost constant feasting. A great chief might have several canoes filled with food, challenging the crowd to eat everything.

On the last day, the village speaker gave out gifts in the name of the host. The most important guests received the most elaborate presents. The only exception was in the case of a hated enemy, who was likely to receive the most elegant gifts as a way of showing him up.

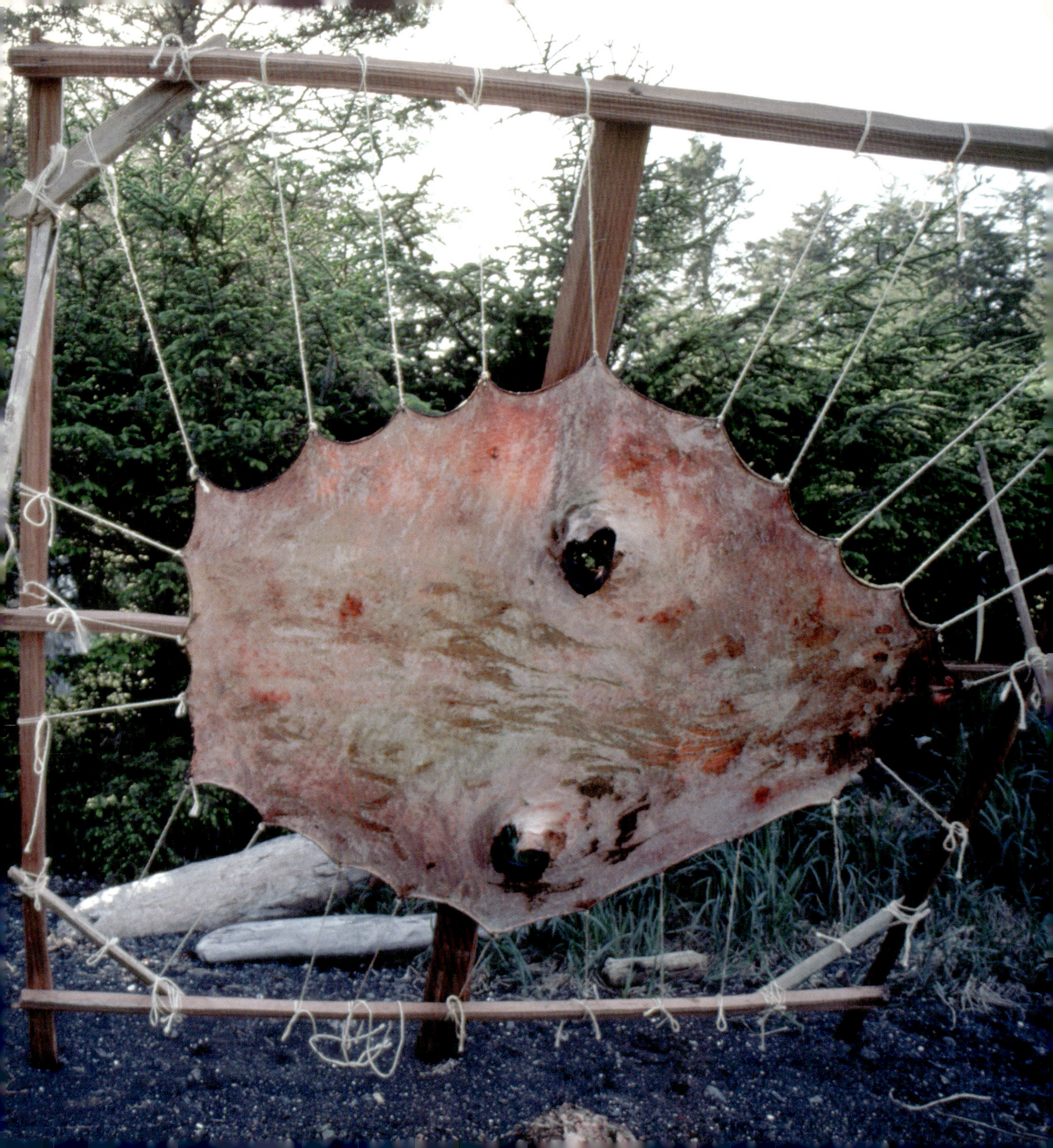

4 · THE HAIDA TODAY

The rich and varied culture of the Haida was almost completely destroyed by the arrival of the Europeans, Americans, and Canadians. European diseases reduced the population to about 20 percent of what it had been in 1600. Entire villages disappeared. In addition, the lure of trade goods such as guns, iron kettles, metal tools, and cloth led to overhunting, destroying the herds of animals that the Haida relied on for much of their food supply. To make matters worse, Russian and American fishing fleets moved into the rivers and bays, taking huge amounts of the salmon and other fish that had been vital to the Indians. From 1500 to 1900, Indian cultures throughout North and South America suffered through similar times of wrenching change and destruction.

By the 1850s, with the discovery of gold in the American

Sealskins were stretched on a frame to dry.

West, the Haida began to lose more and more of their land. Miners, followed by timber companies, claimed more and more territory. To save the Northwest Coast tribes, the U.S. and Canadian governments established reservations or **reserves** for many of the tribes.

Reservation life did little to help the Haida. Because they had lost so much of their fishing, hunting, and gathering, they had to depend on government handouts to survive. Their children were forced to go to government boarding schools, where they were taught English and did not learn about their own culture.

One Haida clan after another gave up its land and moved onto the reservations that were set up by the government. The life of the Haida continued to decline in the 1900s. The U.S. government declared that the Northwest Coast tribes should be allowed to take half the annual catch of salmon and other fish, but **poachers** continued to take most of the catch. In addition, logging companies and salmon-packing factories

Haida elders in traditional costume watch the dedication ceremony for a new canoe.

destroyed large areas of the environment. Beginning in 1948, the environment was altered further when the U.S. Army Corps of Engineers began building dozens of dams to produce electricity. Almost every dam interfered with the spawning of the salmon that were so important to the Haida's traditional way of life.

In the 1960s, the civil rights movement in the United States, spearheaded by African Americans and leaders such as the Reverend Martin Luther King Jr., inspired Native Americans to demand changes that would help them preserve their language and their culture. Some tribes tried to win their rights through court cases; others protested at government offices.

Since the 1960s, more and more Americans and Canadians have come to realize that all Indian societies had received unfair treatment over the years. The Haida and other Northwest Coast Indians began to take renewed pride in their cultural heritage. Although ceremonies based on wealth, such as the potlatch, were no longer possible, other ceremonies and dances were revived. Crafts, especially woodworking, found a new market with the rapid growth of tourism. Many cultural and environmental organizations became very active in demanding protection of Indian rights. The Haida today are rebuilding their way of life with new hope for the future.

TIME LINE

7500 B.C.E.	First evidence of humans living on Northwest Coast.
6000 B.C.E.	Ancestors of modern Northwest Coast Indians were building wood-plank houses.
1600–1700 C.E.	First contact with Europeans.
1670	The English organize the Hudson's Bay Company to trade with the tribes of the Northwest Coast.
1700–1800	English Hudson's Bay Company and Russian traders urge Indians to bring in furs, causing decline in sea otters and forest animals; European diseases cause sharp decline in Indian populations.
1790s	First American ships join Northwest Coast trade.
1799	Russia organizes the Russian American Trading Company to compete with British, Canadian, and American traders.

1800-1900	The Haida give up their lands and move onto reservations.
1824	U.S. government creates Bureau of Indian Affairs.
1867	United States buys Alaska from Russia, including islands on which the Haida live.
1924	Congress passes Citizenship Act, making Indians U.S. citizens.
1960s	Civil rights movement inspires Native Americans to demand their rights.
1968	American Indian Movement organized by Indians to work for Indian rights.
1978	Indian Religious Freedom Act guarantees the right to practice traditional religions.

GLOSSARY

coppers: Thin pieces of copper hammered into thin plaques and decorated with engraved designs.

cradleboard: A stiff piece of wood on which infants were strapped and carried around while their mothers worked.

household: Related families living in the same house.

poacher: Someone who kills or takes game or fish illegally.

potlatch: A feast during which the host gave away much of his wealth to demonstrate his importance.

reservations: Areas of land set aside by the U.S. government as a home for Native American tribes.

reserve: The Canadian term for "reservation."

shamans: Men who had special powers for healing the sick.

vision quest: A teenage boy's journey to find his special sign or animal symbol to guide him in his life.

weir: A fish trap made of poles and a net stretched across a river.

FIND OUT MORE

Books

Blackman, Margaret B. *During My Time: Florence Edenshaw Davidson: A Haida Woman*. Seattle: University of Washington Press, 1992.

Collison, Frank, ed. *Yakoun, River of Life*. British Columbia: Council of the Haida Nations, 1990.

Eastman, Carol M. *Gyaehlingaay: Traditions, Tales, & Images of the Kaigani Haida*. Seattle: Burke Museum Publications, 1991.

MacDonald, George. *Haida Art*. Vancouver: Douglas & McIntyre, 1996.

Reid, Martine. *Myths and Legends of Haida Indians of the Northwest: The Children of the Raven*. Santa Barbara, CA: Bellerophon Books, 1988.

Taylor, Colin F. *The American Indian Peoples*. Philadelphia: Courage Books, 2002.

Web Sites

www.alaskan.com/akencinfo/haida.html
www.bcbooks.com/mythshaida.html
www.tlingit-haida.org

About the Author

David C. King is an award-winning author who has written more than forty books for children and young adults, including *Projects About Ancient Egypt* in the Hands-On History series. He and his wife, Sharon, live in the Berkshires at the junction of New York, Massachusetts, and Connecticut.

INDEX

Page numbers in **boldface** are illustrations.

map, 6

African Americans, 40
Alaska, 5–7, **6**, 43
American Indian Movement, 43
Americans, 8–9, 37–38, 42–43
ancestors, 8, 42
Animal People, 10, **11**

Babyland, 27, 28
beliefs, 10–11, 27-28, 29, **32**
Bureau of Indian Affairs, 43

Canadians, 9, 37, 42
canoes, 8, 21, 35, **39**
cemeteries, 23, 27, 32
ceremonies, 5, 27, 31–35, **34**, **39**, 40
children, 27, 28, **28**
Citizenship Act, 43
civil rights movement, 40, 43
clan, 15–17, **15**, **16**, 38
clothing, 17–18, **18**, 19, **39**
coppers, 22, **22**, 44
cradleboard, 27, 44
crafts, 21–23, **22**, **23**, **26**, 28, 32, 41
    project, 24–25

disease, 9, 37, 42

environment, 6–7, 37–41
Europeans, 8–9, 37, 42
fishing, 5, 7–8, 13, 28, 37–38
food, **12**, 13–14, 19-21, 34-35, 37
    recipe, 20

government, 16, **16**
    of Canada, 9, 38
    charity, 9, 38
    of United States, 9, 38, 43
history, 8–9, 23, 31, 37–38, 42–43
household, 15, 31, 44
houses, 7, 8, 14-15, 17, 42
Hudson's Bay Company, 42
hunting/gathering, 5, 7–8, 13–14, 21, 28, 37–38

Indian Religious Freedom Act, 43
Indian rights, 40–41, 43

King, Martin Luther Jr., 40

land, 4, 5–7, **6**, 9, 37–38, 43

marriage, 29, 31

Northwest Coast Indians, 5, 17–18, 21, 30, 38, 40, 42

old age/death, 31–33, **33**
poacher, 38, 44
population data, 7, 9, 37, 42
potlatch, 33–35, **34**, 41, 44
Prince of Wales Island, 6
religion, 29–30, 43
reservation, 9, 38, 43, 45
reserve, 38, 45
Russians, 8, 37, 42–43
Russian Trading Company, 42
salmon, 7, 13, 19, 37–38, 40
sea otter, 8-9, 42
shaman, 29, 30, **30**, 45
totem pole, 15, **15**, 17, 23, 24–25, 27
trade, 8–9, 22, 37, 42

U.S. Army Corps of Engineers, 40
villages, 6, **14**
vision quest, 29, **32**, 45
wealth, 9, 16, **22**, 31, 33, 40
weir, 13, 45
woodworking, 5-6, 15, 21, 23–24, **23**, 28, 41
wool dogs, 18

48